# LITTLECOTE - PART 1
# A History of Inheritance

Lying in the meadowland of the beautiful Kennet valley, to the west of Hungerford and close by the village of Chilton Foliat, is Littlecote. Now a country house hotel, owned by Warner Holidays, this Elizabethan house has an intriguing history. Once the focus of a much larger estate, Littlecote was described over 400 years ago by John Leland, the first English antiquary, in his *Itinerary* as...

*'a right faire and large parke hangynge upon the clyffe*
*of a highe hille welle woddyd over Kennet'*

## Love, murder, scandal and romance

The house and its setting presents a marvellous sense of tranquillity which belies the turmoil of some of its former inhabitants. From its conception in Edward I's reign, up until its formal sale to Sir Ernest Wills in 1929, Littlecote passed by various forms of inheritance through the de Calstone, Darrell and Popham families. Accompanying these inheritances are tales of love, murder, scandal and Royal romance .

It was here that Henry VIII courted Jane Seymour, and that 'Wild' William Darrell, accused of two murders, brought an end to the Darrell inheritance of Littlecote. The circumstances of the acquisition or inheritance by Judge Popham, later Lord Chief Justice who presided over the trails of Walter Raleigh and Guy Fawkes, are shrouded with tales of bribery and corruption.

# ..... *THE INFLUENCE OF THE DARRELLS* .....

The Manor of Littlecote had remained in the de Calstone family, certainly from around 1290, until William Darrell of Yorkshire, Sub Treasurer of England in Richard II's reign, married Elizabeth, daughter and heiress of Thomas de Calstone, in 1415 and inherited the estate. Their son Sir George Darrell...*'espoused the Yorkist cause and became Keeper of the Great Wardrobe to Edward IV'*

On his death in 1474, the Estate was in trust for his infant son, Edward, and included the Archbishop of Canterbury amongst the trustees. Later, as Sir Edward, he served as High Sheriff of Wiltshire in 1512 and became Vice-Chamberlain to Queen Katherine of Arragon. As Keeper of her Park of Chilton Foliat he received 10 oaks in 1530, the year before he died, suggesting that building operations were in hand at Littlecote. These influential connections give us an inkling of the growing significance of Littlecote and of the important characters of the day who may have been received within its walls.

# ..... AND A ROYAL LOVE MATCH .....

The first recorded Royal visit took place in 1520 when Henry VIII visited Littlecote on the 18th August, and it was at Littlecote that the King later courted Jane Seymour, a relative of the Darrells. They were married at her father's house, Wulf Hall, not far from Littlecote on May 20th, 1536, the day after Queen Anne Boleyn was beheaded.

Their love is immortalised in a roundel in the high window of the Great Hall, where their initials are united by lovers' knots and cupid's head. Their marriage did not, however, last long. Jane died shortly after the birth of Henry's only male heir, the future Edward VI.

# ..... THE BEGINNINGS OF SCANDAL .....

This Royal connection must have furthered the importance of Littlecote and the influence of the Darrells, but on the death of Sir Edward in 1531, the tide began to change. His grandson, the second Sir Edward, inherited the estate and whittled away the family fortunes with an extravagant lifestyle. He died in 1549 and although his '*household stuff*' at Littlecote was valued at £322 13s. 6d., only £25 of personal property remained after payment of funeral expenses, large debts and extravagant bequests. Edward had preferred the society of a Mary Danyell to that of his wife, Elizabeth, and on his death the most crippling bequest was that of eleven manors to his mistress. Mary claimed an interest in much of the property of Littlecote and after the remarriage of Edward's widow, she maintained herself as the lady of Littlecote and filled the role of wicked step mother to his son William, then aged ten, until he came of age eleven years later.

The north front of the medieval house

# ..... 'WILD DARRELL' .....

It is this son, William who gained himself such an infamous reputation that he later became known as 'Wild Darrell'. He appeared to have inherited his father's interest in female friends. His friendship with the wife of Sir Walter Hungerford was described as *'the prime cause of all his later troubles'*.....

*'This was the crisis of Darrell's fortunes, and he sank beneath it. He was overwhelmed with debt, he was formally accused of one murder, and suspected of another; he had to bear the odium of debauchery and fraud, he was at law with nearly all his tenants, and in a state of open warfare with most of his neighbours; finally he had been thrown into gaol and compelled to promise an enormous bribe, £3000 at least of our money, to the Lord Lieutenant of his county, the needy courtier Pembroke.....his own kinsman, in order to obtain his release.'*
(Hubert Hall, Society in the Elizabethan Age, 1887)

He was not apparently found guilty of an affair with Sir Walter Hungerford's wife as the evidence of witnesses, all from Farleigh Castle - the seat of Sir Walter Hungerford, was not accepted by the judges.

Darrell did not choose an easy path and was imprisoned for a short time in the Fleet in 1579 for slandering the queen in a dispute with Sir Henry Knyvet. Incessant litigation arising partly from his father's will and his own minority made him enemies. Accusations of infanticide and murder were made against him and he was again indicted at Marlborough assizes in 1588 for slandering the sovereign.

## ..... *MURDER* .....

## *The Littlecote Murder Tradition*

Darrell had been accused of being an accessory to a murder committed by a servant. This case may have been the origin of the Littlecote murder tradition, but the most notorious murder story associated with Littlecote, though never proven, concerned the murder of a new-born baby, of which various accounts exist.

In 1575, a midwife called Mother Barnes residing in Shefford was roused at night and offered a high reward if she would attend a lady who needed her midwifery skills. The night was clear and the moon at the full, so that the midwife could discern the messenger was of gentle blood. He told her that she must be blindfolded and mount the pillion behind him. The proffered fee prevailed, she submitted to the terms and the bandage was not removed until she was in the bedroom of her patient, the furnishings of which signified a grand house. Tradition also avers to her patient having been masked.

After successfully delivering a boy, she was ordered by a ferocious wild-eyed man to hurl the baby into a fire. The midwife pleaded with the man to allow her to keep the baby, and bring it up as her own but the man would not agree and the baby was burnt to death, though who committed it to the fire is not clear.

Other versions tell of the murder of the baby by the man who had brought her to the bedside and then its burning in the fire of the bed chamber. On the following night the midwife was again blindfolded, placed on the pillion and put down at her cottage door.

# ..... *THE MIDWIFE'S CONSCIENCE* .....

The midwife's conscience eventually got the better of her bribe. Through recollections of the kind of road they seemed to travel, the apparent distance, the water they forded and above all the piece of the bed-hangings which she had cut away and secreted as she watched by the bedside, she identified the house as Littlecote and the wild-eyed man as 'Wild' William Darrell. 'Wild Darrell' was tried and despite the evidence against him was, according to which account is heard, found guilty but was pardoned or was found not guilty by the Judge. Legend has it that later, upon Darrell's death, the Judge inherited Littlecote. The inheritor was in fact Judge John Popham, a relative of Darrell's.

# ..... HAUNTINGS .....

The identity of the mother of the murdered baby is variously recorded as an unknown woman who died shortly after, or perhaps Lady Knyvett. Sir Henry Knyvett suspected his wife to be the mother of a child, of whose murder, he wrote in 1578, ' *the brute increaseth fowlely*'. Whatever fate befell this hapless women after the birth of her ill fated child, it is she who is said to haunt both the bedroom and the landing beyond where the foul deed was done. Some accounts record the bedroom being adjacent to the Diamond Hall on the ground floor.

The Haunted Landing and Fireplace and a glimpse of the Haunted Bedroom beyond

# ..... WILD DARRELLS DECLINE .....

This *'sinister legend of 'Wild Darrell', dug up by Aubrey a century later, in his Lives of Eminent Men, and embellished by Scott in* Rokeby *cannot be altogether baseless'*.

Aubrey suggests that

> *'the knight was brought to his tryall; and to be short, this judge had his noble house, parke and mannor, and (I thinke) more, for a bribe to save his life.'*

However, this story does not stand up to close scrutiny as Sir John Popham was not the judge at William Darrell's trial. He was certainly a solicitor, and 'Mr. Attorney' at the time of the crime. Darrell had no 'heir apparent' and it was probably in return for Popham's constant legal assistance to William Darrell, and not simply because he was a relative, that he became the beneficiary of Darrell's will. However at the end of all the best murder mysteries there is a little twist, and...

> ... *'it appears that Darrell sold the reversion to the judge in 1586'*.

Reversion in this instance was the passing of possession of the estate at an appointed time back to the grantor, the Judge, to whom the property had been legally transferred.

## Darrell's Style

William Darrell died in 1589 in a riding accident on the Estate, at a place known as 'Darrell's Leap'. He was apparently riding 'hell for leather' in true character when his horse failed a jump and he fell, breaking his neck, hence the other name for this place, 'Darrell's Style'.

# ..... *THE POPHAM INHERITANCE* .....

John Popham took up residence and in August 1601 received Queen Elizabeth I at Littlecote. He had, as Attorney-General, officiated at the trial of Mary, Queen of Scots, at Fotheringay and was knighted and became Lord Chief Justice in 1597, presiding over the trials of Sir Walter Raleigh in 1603, and Guy Fawkes, in 1606. In 1882 J.P. Neale noted that...

*'He was esteemed a severe judge in the case of robbers, but his severity was well timed, as it reduced the number of highwaymen who infested the country'.*

# ..... *A NEW LEASE OF LIFE FOR THE HOUSE* .....

Sir John was responsible for much improvement in the house and the gardens of Littlecote and a clue to the extent by which he reshaped the house is suggested by Aubrey's cryptic remark, in his *Brief Lives*, that Popham... *'brought brick building to London'*.

Sir John Popham's Coat of Arms over the South Porch

# ..... *UNREQUITED LOVE* .....

Sir John died in 1607, and his only son Francis died in 1644. The estate then passed to Francis's second son Alexander, his elder son John having died in 1638. John was buried *'with great pomp'* at Littlecote, but not without leaving his mark on Littlecote's social history.

## *The Spanish lady*

An old ballad describes the unrequited love of a wealthy and beautiful Spanish lady who fell in love with John when she was placed in his custody after being taken prisoner during a raid on a Spanish town. She begged to come to England with him and offered him her fortune, but he declined, saying...

> *'I in England already have*
> *A sweet woman to my wife*
> *I will not falsify my vow for gain*
> *Not for all the fair dames that live in Spain'*

to which she replied

> *'Oh how happy is that woman*
> *That enjoys so true a friend*
> *Many happy days God send her*
> *Of my suit I make an end*
> *On my knees I pardon crave*
> *For my offence*
> *From which love and true affection did commence.'*

Her portrait, painted in 1623 and attributed to Zuccaro, once hung at Littlecote.

# ..... AND A PLACE IN CIVIL WAR HISTORY .....

Alexander was a member of Parliament for Bath and became a Colonel in the Parliamentary Army.  He spent most of the period of the Civil War away from Littlecote with his troops, but he prudently returned with some 60 armed cavalry troopers to escort his wife to a place of safety away from the defenceless Littlecote just before war was formally declared.

The Cromwellian Guardroom

# ..... 'DROPPING OFF' IN CHAPEL .....

He was responsible for the creation of the Cromwellian Chapel, which he had remodelled during the Civil War from what is believed to be the former medieval hall. It is the only remaining example of a Cromwellian chapel in a private house, with the pulpit positioned where the alter would be in other places of worship. The term 'dropping off' originates from the design of the pews which were so constructed that anyone falling asleep in them would literally slip off the gently sloping, polished seat.

# ..... *THE GREATEST CIVIL WAR ARMOURY* .....

Until recently, the Great Hall housed the most complete collection of Civil War armour, buff-coats and firearms in the country, originally worn and used by the Littlecote garrison of the Parliamentary Army. The collection was bought by the Royal Armories in 1985 to safeguard its long-term survival, and initially it remained on splendid display at Littlecote. In 1996 the collection was removed to the new Royal Armories Museum in Leeds. However, with the reopening of Littlecote in 1997, Warner Holidays hope that much of the original display will be returned to its rightful home to once more grace the walls of the Great Hall.

# ..... *A ROYAL PARDON* .....

After the Civil War, Colonel Popham joined with General George Monck in helping to restore Charles II to the throne, and was elected a member of the Council of State which administered the Government between the dissolution of the Long Parliament and the Restoration of the Monarchy. He received a Royal Pardon and on the 1st September, 1663 he entertained Charles II and Queen Katherine to *'a costly dinner'* at Littlecote during the King's Royal Progress to Bath.

Thus the Royal blessing secured the future and fortunes of Littlecote which was to remain in the Popham family for a further 266 years.

## *William of Orange slept here*

The importance of the Pophams and of Littlecote was seen again with the visit of William of Orange during his progress from Salisbury to London to take the throne. He retired to Littlecote for two nights after his conference with the commissioners of James II at Hungerford on December 8th, 1688, where a great assemblage including peers and generals was invited to meet him in the Great Hall.

He was accommodated in the north west corner of the house which no doubt provided self contained and secure quarters within the great house. His room subsequently became known as the 'William of Orange Bedroom' within which was hung a large tapestry, one of a set of 60 made for William in Brussels between 1675 and 1700. The tapestry showed Hercules and Apollo as supporters of his Arms as King of England.

# ..... *QUIETER TIMES* .....

With the arrival of the 18th century, the inhabitants of Littlecote enjoyed quieter, less contentious lives in these more peaceful times. However, Littlecote remained with the Pophams until the death without issue of Francis Popham in 1804, whereupon the manor passed to Edward William Leyborne, the nephew of Francis, who had died in 1780. Edward added the Popham name to his own.

The arrival of Edward and his wife Elizabeth in 1804 was fortuitous, for it was their sensitive restoration works around 1810 which conserved the beauty of this great house.

The house remained with the Leyborne-Pophams until 1929. However, the family has ceased to reside at Littlecote by the end of the 19th century, the house being let to tenants. One of these tenants, Mr Watney, was responsible for restoring and decorating a number of rooms in appropriate taste, possibly in the hope of acquiring the property.

Sir Ernest Wills, became the tenant in 1922 and had the good fortune to purchase the manor and nearly everything in it in 1929, and remained its devoted possessor until 1958. The house then passed to his son, Major George Wills who in turn transferred the ownership to David Seton Wills in 1968.

The Wills family connection ended with the sale to Peter de Savary in 1985, at which the house, gardens and park became a significant tourist attraction whose theme reflected the history of the house and was encapsulated in the title...

*'Littlecote - the Land that's Trapped in Time'.*

# *LITTLECOTE - PART II*
# *A History of the Settlement*

Long before the building of a manor at Littlecote there had been human activity by the sweet waters of the Kennet, evidenced by finds of Palaeolithic and Mesolithic flint tools, Neolithic flint implements, Bronze Age pottery fragments and a Bronze Age pin head. It is perhaps no wonder that the site also appealed to the Romans, who built here close by the roads from Silchester to both Cirencester and Bath, and to the later inhabitants of the medieval settlement which developed over part of the Roman villa site.

## *A unique discovery*

In 1728 an archaeological discovery, unique in Britain, was made by William George, steward of Littlecote, although the site afterwards was re-buried and its importance was not fully realised until re-excavations took place between 1977 and 1980. The steward's discovery was that of a highly decorative mosaic floor, dating back to Roman times. The central feature of the mosaic pattern represents the musician-priest Orpheus surrounded by the four seasons; possibly Aphrodite with her mirror (Spring), Nemesis or Leda holding a swan (Summer), Demeter the Earth Mother with a vine staff (Autumn) and her daughter Persephone in a draped cloak (Winter). It is thought that this imagery portrays the myths of Dionysus, relevant to the Neoplatonic cult of Orpheus, and that this was the floor of an Orphic Hall used for philosophical and religious ceremonies, which was developed soon after AD 360 from a redundant third century barn.

The Orphic Hall presents a striking architectural plan of a style common to the eastern empire but not seen elsewhere in Roman Britain.

# ..... *THE ROMAN SETTLEMENT* .....

Further excavations and discoveries revealed a broad section of Roman road alongside the river, which is thought to have been constructed soon after the invasion of Britain in AD43, as an early supply route. Some twenty years later it appears that a native settlement of round dwellings and rectangular barns and possibly a shrine developed adjacent to the road at Littlecote. This village may have survived for around one hundred years until it was demolished to prepare for the building of a Roman villa at Littlecote. The villa, a farmhouse of a privately-owned Romano-British agricultural estate, was most likely a two-storey construction of flint block walls with a tiled roof. Within the villa there was a suite of baths including damp heat like a Turkish Bath and dry heat like a sauna. These rooms would have had tessellated and mosaic floors. The remains of the Orphic Hall and the villa have remained exposed to view since 1980 and emphasise the rich and ancient history of Littlecote.

# ..... THE ORPHEUS MOSAIC .....

The Orpheus mosaic tapestry executed by the wife of William George.

# ..... *A MEDIEVAL SETTLEMENT* .....

The next period of settlement at Littlecote was that of a medieval village developed in the 13th and 14th centuries over part of the Roman site with the outlines of medieval cottages seen to the south of the villa, beyond the boundary wall and the well. This village was possibly contemporary with the establishment of the early manor house which is also thought to date back to the 13th century.

Records indicate that the manor of Littlecote was held by Roger de Calstone, of Calstone near Calne, at the time of his death around 1292, and that in 1341 his son Roger received a licence for mass to be said in the oratory of his manor house of Littlecote. Architectural historians have theorised that the existing chapel may have been formed from this oratory which may itself have been the hall of the original manor house. It is also suggested that the range to the west of the chapel was built on the site of the solar wing of the original house.

## *The Sport of Kings*

The early manor house of the de Calstones was expanded in the 15th century, probably by Sir George Darrell, to form a quadrangle to the south of what is now the chapel. It would also appear that the village was swept away at the same time to make way for a deer park to provide sport for the Lord of the Manor, which reflects the increasing importance and fortunes of the family.

This importance is confirmed in the early 16th century, for it is in this park in 1520 that Henry VIII had...

*'goodly pastimes and continual hunting'.*

# ..... CONCEIVED BY SIR EDWARD DARRELL .....

It is with the later Darrells and Pophams that the house would be so greatly expanded to form the splendid Elizabethan mansion which *'must be placed very high among the few that preserve their authentic character.'* (4)

The expansion would appear to have been conceived by Sir Edward Darrell and is supported by the grant of 10 oaks by Queen Katherine in 1530. The grand plan was for a quadrangular mansion to the east of the medieval manor house, which continued to be lived in whilst the work was carried out by both the second Sir Edward and then by his son 'Wild Darrell'.

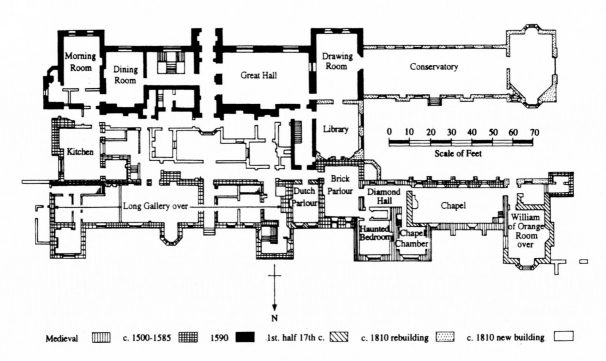

Plan of the ground floor

# ..... *A TUDOR MANSION* .....

The work appears long drawn out, no doubt due to the extravagant lifestyle of the former and the litigation of the latter.  The contract to build the north range, containing the long gallery, is dated 1583.  By 1585 the garden walls to the south and the gate house, centred on the south porch, had been built.  The completion of these items before that of the south front suggests that the foundations of the south range were perhaps in place by the time of 'Wild Darrells' death in 1589.

The north front completed by 'Wild Darrell'

# ..... *FINALLY REALISED BY JOHN POPHAM* .....

It was Sir John Popham who, on inheriting the property in 1590, finally brought order to it and realised the quadrangular plan. He gave the house the Great Hall, entrance and parlours it had been lacking for sixty years and may possibly have used foundations constructed by 'Wild Darrell'. This could account for the speed of completion and the character of the south front being considered somewhat conservative for its time. Whether the works were simply completed or encased by him, he left his mark of style upon the property. Whereas the first Sir Edward used flint and brick rubble, possibly from demolished buildings, Sir John Popham worked entirely in two inch brick, now beautifully mellowed, which gained him the reputation for bringing.. *'brick buildings to London'*.

Littlecote from the south east around 1660-70 by Thomas Wijk

# ..... AND THEN LITTLE ALTERED .....

Over the next two hundred years there were several periods when building alterations occurred. In the first half of the 17th century what is believed to be the hall of the medieval house was converted into a Cromwellian chapel and during the mid 18th century the south side of the west court was rebuilt to full height replacing the single storey seen in the painting by Thomas Wijk.

The north front in 1806 by Buckler

# ..... *THE LEYBORNE INHERITANCE* .....

The next period of development of the house came when Edward Leyborne Popham inherited the property in 1804 and married Elizabeth Andrew in 1806. Elizabeth's childhood had been spent in *'the notably artistic milieu of Powderham'* where she was influenced by the passion for architecture of her mother's family. It is likely that whilst Edward, a Colonel in the army, brought practical enthusiasm to the conservation of Littlecote, it was Elizabeth's artistic intelligence which.. *sought to restore Elizabethan character were it had been altered* by the earlier works and ensured that.. *so much of the rambling old mansion (was) preserved so carefully at the same time that it was made tolerably convenient* .

The south front with the new conservatory in 1821 by J P Neale

# ..... *BROUGHT SYMPATHETIC RESTORATION* .....

In 1810 after the whole of the south side and three quarters of the west side of the quadrangle of the medieval manor house was demolished, the conservatory or orangery was rebuilt with tall gothic windows in timber and.. *'in a very tolerable version of Tudor brickwork'*, whilst internally displaying Regency style.

The west range of the main block was also rebuilt, but not that of the medieval house, thus enabling a view of the park to be gained from the new library.

The chapel wing and open west courtyard

# ..... CENTURIES' OLD CONTINUITY .....

As well as this major rebuilding, many external sympathetic repairs to the property were made around this time including, the restoration of the mullioned windows of the east and west gables of the south front and the installation of early 16th century French or Flemish stained glass in the upper portions of the windows in the Great Hall. A further innovation introduced at this time was the insertion of cloister-like corridors around the internal courtyard of the Elizabethan house. Such was the Leyborne-Pophams sensibility to Littlecote's restoration.

It is remarkable that, whilst so many other country seats received Nash's architectural facelifts and Capability Brown's and Repton's sweeping parklands, that the Classical period left hardly a mark on Littlecote and even the Landscape Movement could not destroy its walled garden.

*'The miracle of Littlecote's restoration in 1809-10 was that, notwithstanding extensive innovation, the north and south elevations were kept virtually intact', (2) and that... 'the impression above all given is of centuries' old continuity, of a place as authentically romantic as the circumstances that have produced and preserved it, and which in that respect..... equates Littlecote with the most famous of historic houses.' (3)*

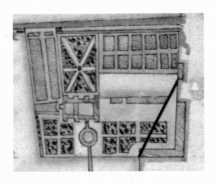

The walled enclosures from Thomas Smith's map of 1775

# ..... *THE FINEST TUDOR BRICK MANSION* .....

*The purist in classic architecture may scorn it as formless, ignorant and rough. But it is amazingly sympathetic, native of the native, a precious and well preserved model of how our rich men housed and rehoused themselves within the teeming Tudor century .* (2)

Perhaps it is this air of native sympathy and harmony which has enabled Littlecote to hold itself above fashionable phases and why its guardians have respected its conceptual styles. It remains *'one of the finest Tudor brick mansions in the land'*.

The north front

# LITTLECOTE - PART III
## The Interior of the Mansion

The house is entered through the south porch which leads on through a very fine Elizabethan screen into the the Great Hall. With a grey and white diamond flagstone floor, oak panelling to the walls and purely English fan-vaulted ceiling, this hall is one of the most splendid of its kind. The impressive quality extends to the large windows which reflect the growing desire in Tudor times to allow the maximum of light and air to enter the house. It is in the high window here that the love-match between Henry VIII and Jane Seymour is immortalised. The hall contains amongst other things, a 30 ft long Shovel-Board Table and the finger stock said to have been used by Judge Popham to confine prisoners in the dock.

# ..... A DUTCH PARLOUR .....

From the north west corner of the Great Hall a door leads into the drawing room with its fine hand painted Chinese wallpaper, and it is from this room that the new rooms created by Edward and Elizabeth Leyborne-Popham are entered. To the west is the conservatory or orangery which once supported exotic vegetation, whilst to the north is the Popham Library with its fine view, through the open courtyard, along the Kennet and up hill to Park Coppice.

Beyond the library is the splendid Dutch Parlour, so named because its painted panels were executed by Dutch prisoners who were taken from a naval battle around 1665 and temporarily housed at Littlecote. Their work depicts scenes from 'Don Quixote' and Butler's 'Hudibras', as well as more typical scenes from domestic life.

# ..... IN THE MEDIEVAL HOUSE .....

Next to the Dutch Parlour is the Brick Parlour which, until recent times, had its floor strewn with scented rushes collected from the nearby water meadows, a custom dating back to medieval times. This room contains unusual and very fine 17th century panelling behind which a secret passage is said to be hidden. Beyond the Brick Parlour is the Diamond Hall, off which is the other room that some versions of the Littlecote murder suggest was the place of confinement of the unfortunate woman and the murder of her child.

The Diamond Hall leads through into the Cromwellian Chapel, and stairs at the west end of the chapel lead up to both the chapel gallery and on to the William of Orange bedroom, which is now somewhat isolated from the remainder of the house. When King William slept here the range on the west side of the medieval courtyard still existed. The gallery in the chapel also leads back to the more popular location of the haunted landing and the haunted bedroom.

# ..... THE JERUSALEM STAIRCASE .....

To the east of the Dutch Parlour is a corridor which was once an entrance from the east courtyard. The Cromwellian guard room is adjacent to this entrance and protected the Jerusalem stairs which were used during the Civil War to reach the garrison dormitory.

The staircase is an interesting spiral with treads formed by solid blocks of oak some 5 ft wide. With their solid, robust character one could almost imagine that 'Wild Darrell' anticipated the existence of a garrison at Littlecote. The main purpose of the staircase was, however, as a means of access to the principal feature of 'Wild Darrell's north range, the Long Gallery.

# ..... *THE LONG GALLERY* .....

Completed by 'Wild' Darrell, this Long Gallery, 110 feet by 18 feet, is one of the finest in England. Its entrance door is only modest, and is designed to contrast with the sheer size of the room and splendours of the oak panelling and plaster work ceiling. Long galleries were a typical feature of houses at this time. They provided the opportunity for taking exercise without having to venture outdoors in bad weather.

The Jerusalem stairs lead up to the dormitory which lies above the Long Gallery. This is where the Littlecote Garrison was quartered during the Civil War, and it is in this part of the house that heavy footsteps are said to be frequently heard, lending a sinister feeling which recalls the grim and violent times of the Civil War.

# LITTLECOTE - PART IV
# The Gardens and the Park

*'When we pass outward into the gardens, and feel all the sweetness that belongs to emerald lawns and green woods, to shady recesses in the pleasance, and to walks where we may linger in the sun, we find interests that are new and suggestions that are valuable. We recognise the relation of garden and house, and feel the beauty of appropriateness in the surroundings of the dwelling.'* (1)

The delight conveyed by this quotation from the turn of the century, still applies today and it is to Edward and Elizabeth Leyborne-Popham that gratitude should be directed for the continued existence of this marvellous 16th century walled garden.

It was Christopher Hussey, who in 1965 noted that...

*The miracle of Littlecote's restoration in 1809-10 was that, notwithstanding extensive innovation, the Tudor (north) and main Jacobean (south) elevations were kept virtually intact with their setting of walled enclosures, and at least the principal rooms preserved or repaired with a minimum fortification'*... and... *'It is even more surprising that the huge rectangle containing the forecourt to the south and the gardens to the north never 'yielded to the hand of taste'. It is true that the Tudor gate house shown on Wijk's perspective standing in front of the forecourt, was replaced, early in the 18th century with wrought iron gates similar to those erected on the north access at the same time. But The Mount, the favoured feature of Jacobean gardens, still exists at the south west corner of the forecourt enclosure.'*

# ..... *WIJK'S PROSPECT* ....

It is known that a deer park was created at the same time as the medieval house and it is assumed that the walled enclosures of the gardens date from the expansion of the house by the Darrells in the 16th century. Certainly the gate house and walls to the south front are known to have been built by 1585. Pictorial evidence of these works is not found until the mid 1660's with the marvellous picture by Thomas Wijk. Within this prospect, Littlecote is raised to the level of great documentary art by the astonishing account of multifarious activities in garden and park. The painting would appear to accurately portray the house and its walled enclosures although the detail to the west of the house is misleading, with the direction of the avenue rising up hill to Park Coppice distorted. This is however, a common artistic device used in landscape painting, compressing a broader scene into the confines of the canvas.

Extract from the Andrews and Dury Map of Wiltshire, 1773

# ..... *AND THE EARLY MAPS* .....

It is not known whether the avenues shown in the Wijk's painting were ever planted. There was certainly an avenue to the east which is shown on the Andrews and Dury Map of Wiltshire, dated 1773, but neither this map nor the estate map made by Thomas Smith of Shrivenham, dated 1775, indicate such avenues. What these documents do confirm is the form of the walled gardens and the changes which occurred during the 17th century.

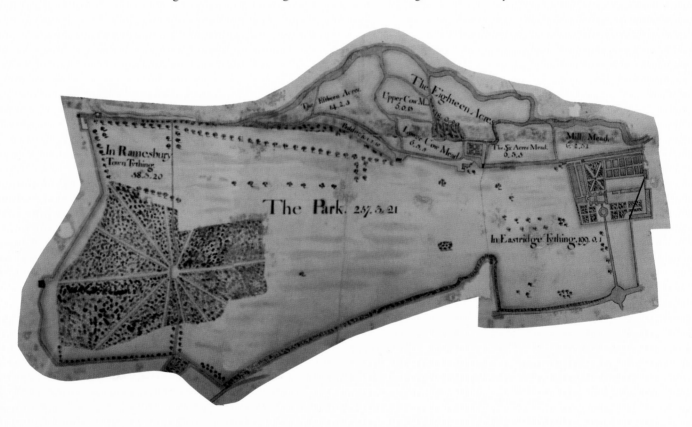

Extract from the Estate map by Thomas Smith of Shrivenham, 1775

# ..... *THE CLAIRVOYEE* .....

The Wijk's painting still shows the gate house, the straight path to the south front and the single storey south range to the medieval west courtyard. By contrast, the two maps clearly show the reforming of the entrance courtyard to the south of the house with the sweeping away of the gate house and the construction of the circular driveway. This was accompanied by reducing the height of the brick wall and replacing instead with wrought iron railings, the whole effect with the gates being termed 'clairvoyee', allowing views out into the park from this enclosure.

The Andrews and Dury map also depicts the south elevation which clearly shows the later two storey building to the south of the medieval west courtyard.

Whether the avenues in the Wijk's painting were real or simply an intention, the alterations to the Parkland around 1810, though not extensive, replaced this Renaissance character with a more picturesque vision with clumps of parkland trees. Despite this, the eleven radiating rides within Park Coppice on the hill to the west were retained.

# ..... *NEVER 'YIELDED TO THE HAND OF TASTE'* .....

Within the walled gardens the extent to which the use of these walled enclosures changed in the early 19th century is not clear. What is gratifying is their survival, despite the prevailing system of improvement which swept away many old fashioned walled gardens in the affluent and romantic period of the late 18th century. As late as 1886 the 1st Edition of the 25 inch Ordnance Survey map shows the original compartmentation of the enclosures to the south of the house remaining, with the central enclosure still occupying an area no wider than that of the new house, which was the fashion in Sir John's time. However, the walls which separated this forecourt from a wilderness to the east and a privy garden to the west, may have been removed. The privy garden still existed with the south and west walls maintaining the privacy of the enclosures, whilst the raised terrace or mount at the west end allowed views out over the surrounding park.

It is only within the present century that the south front has been given a more expansive setting. The shrubberies and flower beds of the privy garden and many of the trees in the wilderness have gone, replaced by velvety lawns.

The Mount

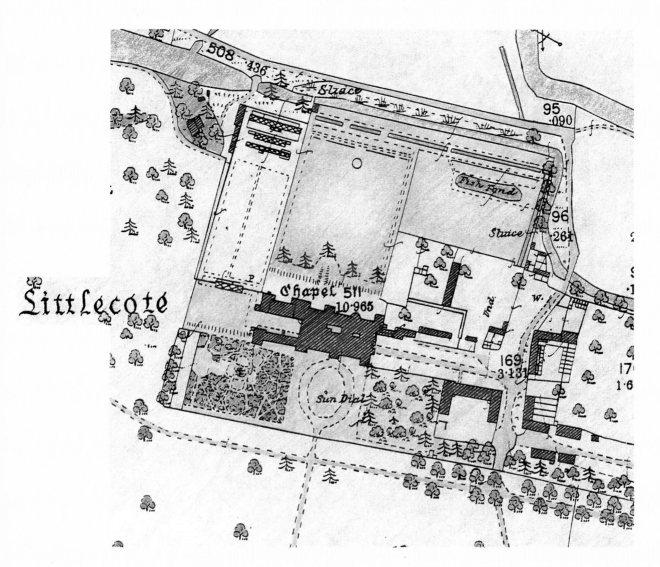

Extract from the 1st Edition 25 inch Ordnance Survey, 1886

# ..... *AND EARLY 20TH CENTURIES* .....

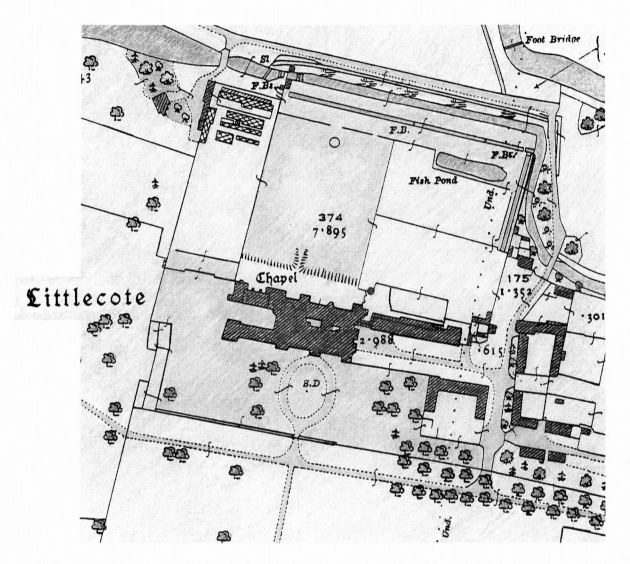

Extract from the 3rd Edition 25 inch Ordnance Survey, 1924

# ..... A STATELY DRIVE OF GREAT ELMS.....

The approach to the house from the east was along a stately drive of great elms which was described by J. C. Loudon, in the Botanical Magazine of May 1834, as... *30 ft wide and a furlong in length which brings the stranger to the enriched iron gates in front of the venerable mansion*. These are the trees seen on the Andrews and Drury map and they still existed well into the present century, despite a description in the Journal of Horticulture and Cottage Gardener of 1866 which describes the trees as... *'very old Elms, now going fast to decay'*.

Within the walled garden to the north of the house the walled enclosures appear to have remained unaltered, whilst softer boundaries of yew and holly hedges have come and gone. Likewise, herbaceous borders have been created then disappeared whilst formal schemes of rose beds, herbaceous plantings and bedding displays have been a constant feature at the north end of the great lawn.

## *glorious borders of herbaceous flowers*

The letting of Littlecote to tenants at the turn of the century led to works of... *'an appropriate character'* within the house and a description of the gardens would also suggest that these were well cared for...

*'Now, simplicity is the dominant characteristic of the place. There is enclosure by walling and hedges, and every wall is well used as the support for fruit trees or climbing flowers. The Kennet lends a branch of its gentle stream on the north side to form a trout water in the gardens and level meadows, and there are well kept grass walks on either side, flanked by glorious borders of herbaceous flowers.'* (1)

# ..... *GARDENS DESCRIBED IN 'COUNTRY LIFE'* .....

These glorious borders were the product of the tenant, Mr Gerald Lee Bevan, and his wonderful gardener, Glasheen and it is these borders which were taken over by Sir Ernest and Lady Wills in 1922 and long maintained in that condition. The house and gardens were described in the pages of 'Country Life' on three separate occasions in 1902, 1927 and over 4 issues in 1965.

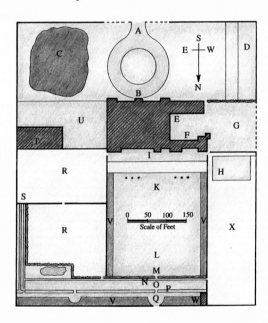

Sketch plan of the Gardens in 1927

**A**, the entrance through wrought-iron clairvoyee; **B**, the porch; **C**, groups of tall trees; **D**, the raised terrace or bowling-green; **E**, the conservatory addition; **F**, the wing containing the old chapel; **G**, the west garden; **H**, the grass plat; **I**, the grass terrace in front of the north facade; **K**, the sloping lawn with a few old Irish yews; **L**, site of lily pool and rose garden; **M**, main way through the topiary hedge; **N**, paved path; **O**, broad band of grass; **P**, canal; **Q**, wrought-iron gate; **R**, vegetable gardens; **S**, return arm of the canal; **T**, stable building; **U**, yards; **V**, principal herbaceous borders; **W**, Garden House; **X**, section for glass-houses, etc.

# ..... *RESURGENCE* .....

Sadly, by 1983 the gardens appear to have lost much of their character with the herbaceous borders greatly reduced in extent and the flower and rose beds grassed over. However, with the arrival of Peter de Savary in 1985, the gardens once again received loving attention and the herbaceous borders were brought back to life. New gravel paths were laid down creating strong vistas through the gateways in the northern walled enclosures and a series of five intricate knot gardens in box were planted along the north front, which now look so characteristic of the house that one would believe they had always been there.

The Great Lawn and the North Front in 1983

# ..... AND AN ASSURED FUTURE .....

Now, with a fine lime avenue once again lining the main drive from the east, the resurgence of the gardens and with new plantings planned for the parkland, the description from 1901 appears most apt...

*'Littlecote belongs to a great class of our old dwelling places.....finally, when we pass away by the avenue through the park we feel that we are leaving one of those places which are landmarks in the life of the English people.'* (1)

The Entrance Gates and the Clairvoyee

# ..... *SEVEN CENTURIES OF SUCCESSION* .....

|  | | | |
|---|---|---|---|
| | **Durnford** | | Manor primarily held by the Durnford family between the late 12th and the mid 13th century |
| | **Roger de Calstone** | | Died c. 1292. Held the manor of Littlecote. |
| *1292* | **Roger de Calstone** | (son) | Died c. 1342. Received a licence for mass to be said in the Oratory of his Manor of Littlecote in 1341. |
| *1342* | **Laurence de Calstone** | (son) | Known to have held the manor in 1356 |
| *1385* | **Thomas de Calstone** | (son) | Manor passed to Thomas by 1385. Died between 1412-19. |
| *1415* | **Elizabeth de Calstone** | (daughter) | Married William Darrell of Yorkshire. |
| *1464* | **Sir George Darrell** | (son) | Became Keeper of the Great Wardrobe to Edward IV. |
| *1474* | **Sir Edward Darrell** | (son) | Became Vice Chancellor to Queen Katherine of Arragon. |
| *1531* | **Sir Edward Darrell** | (gr'dson) | Died 1549 leaving large debts. |
| *1549* | **William Darrell** | (son) | 'Wild Darrell'. Came of age in 1560, accused of murdering a child in 1575, died 1589 in a riding accident. |
| *1589* | **Sir John Popham** | | Died 1607. Attorney General and later Lord Chief Justice. |
| *1607* | **Sir Francis Popham** | (son) | Died 1644. His eldest son John died before him and was buried with great pomp at Littlecote. |
| *1644* | **Alexander Popham** | (2nd son) | Colonel in Parliamentary Army. Helped restore Charles II to the throne in 1660 and received a Royal Pardon in 1663. |
| *1669* | **Sir Francis Popham** | (son) | Died 1674. |
| *1674* | **Alexander Popham** | (son) | Died 1705. |
| *1705* | **Alexander Popham** | (uncle) | Died 1705. |
| *1705* | **Francis Popham** | (son) | Died 1735. |
| *1735* | **Edward Popham** | (son) | Died 1772. |
| *1772* | **Francis Popham** | (son) | Died 1780. |
| *1780* | **Dorothy Popham** | (wife) | Died 1797. Manor devised to reputed son of Dorothy's husband Francis who had died in 1780. |
| *1797* | **Francis Popham** | (son?) | Died 1804. |
| *1804* | **Edward W Leyborne-Popham** | (cousin) | Died 1843. Edward was the nephew of Francis d. 1780. |
| *1843* | **Francis Leyborne-Popham** | (son) | Died 1880. |
| *1880* | **Francis W Leyborne-Popham** | (son) | Died 1907. Latterly let house to tenants. |
| *1907* | **Hugh F A Leyborne-Popham** | (brother) | Let the manor in 1922 to Sir Ernest Wills Bt. |
| *1929* | **Sir Ernest Salter Wills, Bt.** | | Died 1958. Purchased the manor from H.F.A.L - Popham. |
| *1958* | **George S. Wills** | (2nd son) | Died 1979. Ownership transferred to D.S.Wills. |
| *1968* | **David Seton Wills** | (son) | Sold Littlecote to Peter de Savary in 1985. |
| *1985* | **Peter de Savary** | | Littlecote developed as a tourist attraction. |
| *1996* | **Warner Holidays Ltd** | | Purchase of Littlecote from Peter de Savary. Warner Holidays Country Hotel opened in June 1997 |